Dear Child of God,

_____

_____

_____

_____

With love from

_____

In memory of my dear mother and father
who taught me about God and His love!

PJM

Wise Words for Little Ones

God is Everywhere

Words by Patricia J. Murphy
Illustrated by Júlia Moscardó

CANDLE
BOOKS

Published by
Candle Books

www.lionhudson.com
Part of the SPCK Group
SPCK, 36 Causton Street, London, SW1P 4ST

ISBN 978 1 78128 415 5

First edition 2023

Acknowledgments
Scripture quotations are taken from the Holy Bible, New Living
Translation, copyright ©1996, 2004, 2015 by Tyndale House
Foundation. Used by permission of Tyndale House Publishers, Inc., Carol
Stream, Illinois 60188. All rights reserved.

A catalogue record for this book is available from the British Library

Produced on paper from sustainable sources

Printed and bound in China, November 2022, LH54

Contents

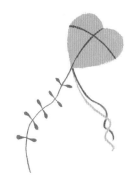

You are a Child of God

Did you know?
Have you heard
the Good News?

While you are
your mother
and father's
pride and joy,

you're also . . .

w a i t f o r i t . . .

a child of God!

7

Before you were born
God picked your parents,
chose your family . . .

and everything about you
from the top of your head
to the tips of your toes!

You are one of God's
greatest creations
from His imagination!

8

You are made from
the greatest joy,
the greatest love,
because

you are a
child of God!

9

Your Heavenly Father
wants only the best for you.

He wants you to live
a life full of love
with all living things!

He wants you to feel
His great love
each and every day,
and everywhere you go.

11

God has big plans
for you!

He wants to help you grow
to become completely
the best self
you can be . . .

the person
He has made
you to be.

To stay in
His light,
to be holy,

because

you are a
child of God!

13

However, if
you should ever
lose your way,
and find yourself
in a dark place.

Or, if you might
do something wrong.

14

He'll help you
make it right.
He will lead you
back to the light.

For there's nothing
you'd ever do
to lose His love.

It's really true!

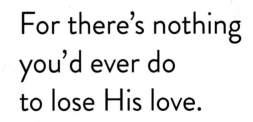

From morning
until night,
for the rest
of your life
and beyond,

God's love will
always and forever
surround you.

No matter what
you say or do,
He'll always
love and
forgive you.

Because you –
the wonderful,
the glorious,
the one-of-a-kind you –
you are His child.

You are a child of God!

Never Fear, God is Near!

When you wake up
to start your day,

head to school

or to play.

18

When you try
something new,
and you don't
know what to do.

Never fear, God is near!

God is always with you,
to cheer you on,
and comfort you.

When your happy
turns into sad,
or good days
turn to bad.

When you are lonely
or you are scared,
and cannot find
your teddy bear.

Never fear, God is near!

He is in
your family,
and your friends,

with a love that never ends.

When you've done
something wrong
or, you need
to be strong.

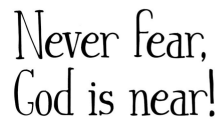

Never fear,
God is near!

His love for you
is shining through . . . you!

You will know what to do.

This is all because
God loves you.

He made you
from great love,
for great love.

Never fear,
God is near!

He has a plan.
He is your
biggest fan!

25

So, talk to Him
and pray
each and
every day.

God bless . . .

Please help me . . .

Share your
worries,
your cares,
and praise.

26

Forgive me . . .

Watch over . . .

Never fear, God is near!

Let Him know
you know He's there.

27

But, if He feels
far away
remember this . . .

God will always be
as close as a whisper

28

and a cool summer breeze.

He'll never leave you
from now until eternity!

Never fear,
God is near!

29

Love God, Love All

Love is . . .

one of God's greatest gifts!

God's word helps you
live in His love.

His word gives you ways
to show Him love
and to share His love.

To love God,
and to love all.

The good news is you can show
your love for God in many ways.

By saying
and singing
God's name in love
and praise.

By getting
to know God,
through reading His word

and discovering
His ways.

By spending
time with God
every day!

By counting blessings,
and giving thanks
for all God has given you.

By celebrating Him together on Sundays, and Holy Days.

To love God, and to love all.

You can show God love, too.
By loving everyone
as much as you love
yourself.

You can do it!

By caring
for the Earth,
all its creatures,
and those in need.

Just like
God loves
and cares for you!

By hurting no living thing
and saying sorry
if you do.

And forgiving someone when they hurt you.

You can do that, too!

Just like God forgives you!

For when you
show God love
and share it, too . . .

you will know more love
than you could ever imagine
and, receive God's grace, too!

Love God, love all.

Memory Verses and Actions

Here are some ways to put these wise words into action . . .

You are a Child of God

Memory verse

See how very much our Father loves us, for he calls us his children, and that is what we are!

1 John 3 verse 1

Tell the world through actions

Tell everyone that you are a child of God – but, try not to use words! Show them with your loving actions. Do special acts of kindness for others without telling them. Say "yes" when someone asks for help and lend a hand or two. Join your parents or carers and volunteer to help people and animals in need.

Celebrate daily

Celebrate every day that you are a child of God! You can do this by praising God's name in prayer or in song, reading the Bible, and attending church regularly. These things will fill your heart and life with joy, and please God, too.

Give thanks

Say prayers of thanks for being a child of God. Say this prayer or make up your own prayers.

> **Dear Heavenly Father, Thank you for making me, choosing me, and loving me as your child. Help me be the best me that I can be! Amen.**

Activity

Use a plain t-shirt and fabric paints or pens to make a special "You are a child of God" t-shirt, or decorate plant pots using permanent markers with these words to give as gifts.

Never Fear, God is Near!

Memory verse

Do not be afraid or discouraged. For the LORD your God is with you wherever you go.
Joshua 1 verse 9

When you are feeling afraid

- Remind yourself with words of encouragement. Repeat "Never fear, God is near!"

- Share your fears with your family and friends. Most of what we fear will never happen!

- Talk to God about your fears and ask God to ease them. With God's help, anything is possible!

Activity

Make a small drawing of something that reminds you of God to keep in your pocket.

Love God, Love All

Activity

Create a Bible bookmark for your Bible to keep your place as you read the Bible throughout the year.

Show love to God

Find different ways to show God your love for Him. Talk to Him when you wake up. Think about God's love to help you make choices throughout the day. Give thanks for His love and count your blessings as you pray at bedtime – or anytime you want to talk to Him.

Show love to others

Treat everyone the way you want to be treated. Smile, speak kindly to others, take turns, help others, say "sorry" when you are sorry, and "I forgive you" when others hurt you. Ask God to help you show love to others.